ALASKA'S
BEARS

Grizzlies, Black Bears, and Polar Bears

Text by Bill Sherwonit

Photographs by Tom Walker

ALASKA NORTHWEST BOOKS™
Anchorage ■ Seattle ■ Portland

For Dulcy, who shares my passion for bears.
And who, like them, has been an important teacher.

ACKNOWLEDGMENTS—I thank the many bear biologists and researchers who have shared their knowledge with me over the years. I'm especially grateful to several of those same biologists who each read portions of the manuscript and provided insights to clarify the text: Steve Amstrup, Larry Aumiller, Gerald Garner, John Hechtel, Sterling Miller, Scott Schliebe, and Chuck Schwartz. I also thank anthropologist and nature writer Richard Nelson for his comments. I greatly appreciate Don Graydon's skilled editing and Ellen Wheat's continuing guidance, encouragement, and discipline. I thank all those who've enthusiastically supported my "writing life," especially Dulcy Boehle. Finally, I honor the bears; they continue to be an inspiration and blessing in my life.

Text copyright © 1998 Bill Sherwonit
Photographs copyright © 1998 Tom Walker

Library of Congress Cataloging-in-Publication Data
Sherwonit, Bill, 1950-

      Alaska's bears / Bill Sherwonit.

        p. cm. — (Alaska pocket guide)

      Includes bibliographical references (p. 91) and index.

      ISBN 0-88240-499-7

      1. Grizzly bear—Alaska. 2. Black bear—Alaska. 3. Polar bear—Alaska.
I. Title. II. Series.
QL737.C27S5 1998
599.78'09798—dc21   97-44559
                                                            CIP

Portions of the brown/grizzly bear and bear-viewing chapters appeared previously in *Alaska Geographic* and *Alaska* magazine, in different form.

PHOTOS—*Front cover* (clockwise): Brown bear sow and cubs; black bear; polar bear. *Back cover:* Grizzly scratching its back. *Pages 1–2, 95–96* (end papers): Polar bear. *3:* Brown bear cubs playing. *5:* Brown bear prints. *6:* Brown bears play-fighting. *12–13:* Polar bear cub and sow. *34–35:* Female brown bear and cubs. *60–61:* Black bear. *80:* Brown bear fishing for salmon.

Originating Editor: Marlene Blessing; Managing Editor: Ellen Wheat; Editor: Don Graydon; Designer: Constance Bollen; Maps: Gray Mouse Graphics.

Alaska Northwest Books™
An imprint of Graphic Arts Center Publishing Company
Catalogs and book orders: P.O. Box 10306, Portland, OR 97296-0306
800-452-3032

Printed on acid- and elemental-chlorine-free recycled paper in the United States of America

CONTENTS

BEAR COUNTRY

^^^

The sight of the bear stirred me like nothing else the country could contain. What mattered was not so much the bear himself as what the bear implied. He was the predominant thing in that country, and for him to be in it at all meant that there had to be more country like it in every direction and more of the same kind of country all around that. He implied a world.

—John McPhee, **Coming into the Country** (1976)

I first saw a wild bear in 1974, during my first month in Alaska. A chocolate-colored grizzly, it stood several hundred yards away, busily digging into the tundra for roots or perhaps ground squirrels. Like John McPhee, I saw the grizzly while exploring the Brooks Range wilderness, though I'd come not as a writer but as a 24-year-old geologist recently out of graduate school. And like McPhee, I was deeply stirred by the sight of this bear. But what moved me was the grizzly itself, rather than anything it implied about wildness or vast, undeveloped landscapes. A fuller appreciation of that connection would come later.

This black bear has left the forest to search the tundra for blueberries.

Even now I can recall the mix of awe, delight, and fear that I felt, the desire to know more about grizzlies. About bears. Still, I couldn't have realized the extent to which bears—both as physical beings and as metaphors—would become a fascination of mine, a passion.

I eventually left Alaska for California, but returned in 1982, now a writer. Two things, above all others, drew me back: wild landscapes and wildlife. I suppose you could say I wanted to be closer to the bear's world and all that implies.

Like many people who live here, I sometimes call Alaska "bear country"—for good reason. Alaska is the only one of our nation's 50 states to be inhabited by all three of North America's ursine species: the black bear, polar bear, and brown bear (also known as the grizzly). The statewide population of each of the three bears is thriving, thanks largely to

Alaska's abundance of wild, remote, and undeveloped regions.

There are few places you can go in Alaska and not share the landscape with bears. Even Anchorage, with its 260,000 people, is visited annually by black and brown bears that inhabit the tundra and forests along its edges. I've discovered that the presence of bears, even if unseen, changes my relationship with a place: it makes me more attentive, more aware of my surroundings.

Alaska offers some of the world's best bear-viewing. Managed programs at places like McNeil River, Brooks Falls, and Admiralty Island give even backcountry neophytes a chance to safely watch wild bears in their natural environments.

As one who loves both bears and literature, I've lined my bookshelves with dozens of bear books. But until now, there hasn't been a book specifically about Alaska's bears that fits the category of field guide, a book that slips easily into a jacket pocket or day pack—and one that also provides entertaining armchair reading for when you're not in bear country. Here, in one pocket-sized edition, is a book that can help you understand Alaska's bears and their natural histories. Chapters on each of the three species cover their physical appearance, behaviors, yearly cycles, ecological niches, and relationships with humans. One chapter looks at Alaska's prime bear-viewing sites, with full details for those who would like to visit. You'll also find tips for traveling safely through bear country. Complementing the text are the photographs of longtime Alaskan Tom Walker, a premier wildlife photographer who has spent hundreds of hours in the company of bears.

Over the past 16 years, I've shared the Alaskan landscape with bears in places that range from lush coastal rain forests to high alpine valleys to arctic tundra meadows. Through these encounters, my respect and admiration for bears—and their world—continues to grow. I've also been lucky enough to meet several of Alaska's foremost bear researchers. The knowledge they've imparted to me, I now share with you, in this guide to Alaska's bears and the wild country they inhabit. ■

Arctic Ocean

Prudhoe Bay

Beaufort Sea

Arctic National
Wildlife Refuge

RANGE

S K A

ARCTIC CIRCLE

Fairbanks

RANGE

UNITED STATES
CANADA

ST. ELIAS RANGE

chorage

CHUGACH
MOUNTAINS

Alaska's brown bears (grizzly bears) range throughout the entire state, except for part of the Yukon–Kuskokwim Delta and many islands. Black bears occupy three-quarters of the state, absent only from unforested mainland regions—the Seward and Alaska Peninsulas, the North Slope, and part of the Yukon–Kuskokwim Delta—and many islands. (See the chapter on polar bears for a map of the range for Alaska's polar bears.)

CANADA

Glacier Bay
National Park
and Preserve

Juneau

Admiralty
Island

Gulf of Alaska

PACK CREEK

Wrangell

ANAN CREEK

Pacific Ocean

Ketchikan

Bear-viewing sites ★

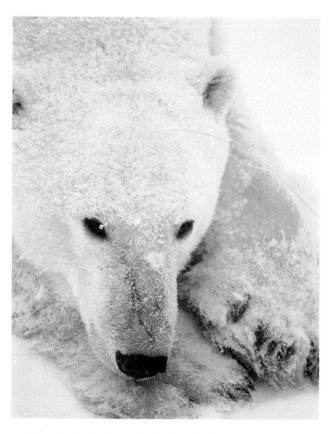

The polar bear's dense, double-layer fur keeps the animal well insulated during arctic blizzards.

I t's strange, at first, to think of any bear as a marine mammal. But the more you learn about the polar bear and its lifestyle, the more you understand why biologists have placed it in a group that includes whales, seals, sea otters, and walrus.

The polar bear's life is so intimately tied to marine environments that some call it the sea bear; even its scientific name, *Ursus maritimus*, recognizes this connection. Others call it the ice bear, the lord of the Arctic. These too fit. Of all the earth's bears, only the polar bear lives exclusively in the Arctic. To be more precise, it is most at home on the Arctic's frozen seas. This is a world that for much of the year is dark and frigid, with icy winds, subzero temperatures, and fierce blizzards. Yet it's here that the polar bear flourishes. As Canadian researcher Ian Stirling puts it: "For thousands of years, the climate, the ice, and the seals upon which it feeds have shaped and finely tuned the evolution of this predator so exquisitely that it has become not just a symbol but the very embodiment of life in the Arctic."

Exactly how the polar bear adapted to the sea-ice environment is still something of a mystery. The species is believed to be a young one, probably only 100,000 to 200,000 years old. It's generally accepted that polar bears evolved from the brown bear line, perhaps along the Siberian coast. This might have happened during the Pleistocene ice age when a population of brown bears became isolated by an advancing glacial sheet. Secluded in an environment filled with seals and no other predatory competitors, these opportunistic feeders discovered a wide-open niche.

The idea of brown bears venturing onto sea ice and learning to hunt seals is not far-fetched. We know that brown bears sometimes feed on seal carcasses and seals that haul out on land. They've occasionally been seen along the Arctic Ocean's edge, not far from basking seals; a few have even been spotted on the sea ice itself, up to 35 miles from land. Given this present-day behavior and the fact that bears are fast learners, it's easy to imagine an isolated group of brown bears gradually adapting to life as seal hunters.

They were successful enough to eventually produce the modern polar bear. Adult male polar bears may weigh up to 1,700 pounds and, standing on their hind legs, reach more than 11 feet high; more commonly, they weigh around 1,000 pounds. Adult females are considerably smaller, rarely weighing more than 600 to 700 pounds.

As generations of sea bears adapted to their new environment and life as a pure carnivore, their bodies went through dramatic change. Teeth became sharper, to help in the shearing of hide, blubber, and meat. Claws that had been long and straight for digging became shorter, sharper, and strongly curved, to permit a better grip on ice and prey. Most noticeably, their fur became a creamy white, to better blend with snow and ice.

More differences from the brown bears: instead of a wide, dish-faced head, polar bears have a long, narrower head with a Roman nose. And they have a much longer neck, which may help them keep their head above water when swimming. Another arctic adaptation is their huge oar-like feet. Combined with partial webbing between the toes, these feet improve the polar bear's swimming ability. And on thin ice, the feet act much like snowshoes, enabling bears to cross ice that a human would break through. On especially weak ice, the bear may spread its legs as wide as possible and crawl on its belly.

Polar bears don't slip on ice, because their footpads are covered with tiny nipple-like projections that increase friction between foot and ice. Also, the soles of their feet have small depressions that may act as suction cups to further improve the bears' grip as they run. Finally, the bottoms of their feet are heavily furred between the toes, which both aids in traction and insulates from the cold.

In contrast with their big feet, polar bears have tiny ears and tails. In that respect they follow a scientific rule-of-thumb that the farther north an animal lives, the smaller its extremities, to conserve body heat.

Polar bears are enthusiastic swimmers. They swim by moving their front paws in dog-paddle strokes, while hind legs help in diving, turning, and other maneuvering. Young bears especially seem to love swimming; but newborn cubs, which have little blubber, cannot remain in cold arctic waters for long or they'll become hypothermic. The blubber of older bears helps in two ways: it insulates from the cold and provides increased buoyancy.

While blubber performs admirably in frigid water and subzero cold, it creates problems when temperatures warm in summer or

Polar bears sometimes sprawl on the ice to keep from overheating.

when a bear exercises hard: polar bears quickly overheat. To regulate body temperature, they have evolved "hot spots" on their face, footpads, inner thighs, and shoulder muscles to dissipate excess heat. To assist this heat loss, bears lie on their back, exposing legs, belly, and feet to the air. Swimming, eating snow, and panting are other ways they cool down. In summer they molt and spend more time resting.

For all their differences, brown bears and polar bears remain enough alike genetically that they can interbreed and produce fertile offspring. Hybrid cubs—produced in captivity—tend to be white at birth and most closely resemble their polar bear parent, but their fur becomes bluish brown or yellowish white with age. There's no evidence, though, that the two species interbreed in the wild.

HOME ON THE ICE

Polar bears are scattered throughout the Northern Hemisphere's region of ice-covered seas, inhabiting the lands

Hoping for a meal, a polar bear inspects a fur seal lair.

and waters of Canada, Greenland, Norway, Russia, and the United States. The best current population estimate is between 21,000 and 28,000.

Until the 1960s, polar bears were believed to be circumpolar nomads that wandered randomly through the Arctic. But close monitoring has radically altered that view. It turns out that polar bears have a seasonal fidelity to certain regions: at any given season, an individual bear is likely to be found in the same area from one year to the next. Exactly how they navigate remains unknown, though it's suspected they may use the position of the sun or stars, or even the earth's magnetic field. With the exception of females raising their cubs, they travel the ice pack alone.

Now, instead of a single circumpolar population, scientists divide polar bears into 16 subpopulations. Alaska's estimated 3,000 to 5,000 polar bears form two distinct subpopulations, though there is some intermingling. About 2,000 live on the Beaufort Sea ice pack; the rest range through the Chukchi and Bering Seas, spending about two-thirds of their time in Russian territory.

The Beaufort population occupies an area of 360,000 square miles off Alaska's northern coast. These bears are long-distance travelers—moving anywhere from 880 to 3,800 miles a year, according to researchers who tracked more than 100 females for a dozen years. (The females were fitted with radio collars and tracked by satellite telemetry. Males haven't been followed because, with necks larger than their heads, the collars fall off.) Single females tended to cover more ground than females constrained by cubs.

The home ranges of individual Beaufort bears varied from 4,900 to as many as 230,000 square miles, an area nearly the size of Texas. Each bear's range overlaps with the ranges of other bears. And because of shifting sea ice and changes in the availability of food, a range's size and shape varies from year to year.

Because polar bears prefer the edges of active ice, where food is most easily accessible, their travel is closely tied to seasonal movements of the ice pack. Beaufort bears move north in the summer and south in the winter as they follow the ice-pack edge, which retreats during the warmer months and then advances as the weather cools. It's intriguing that many of these bears also show an east-west movement, which likely reflects seasonal changes in the distribution of sea ice and open water, changes connected to regional ocean currents.

In the Chukchi and Bering Seas off Western Alaska, the ice pack's leading edge moves nearly 900 miles in a normal year. To stay on the edge, this region's bears have been known to travel from 1,800 to 3,000 miles a year. Radio-tracking data indicates an average home range for Western Alaska polar bears of 96,000 square miles, the largest in the world and more than twice the average for Beaufort Sea bears. And while Beaufort bears

NOT A PARTY ANIMAL

Polar bears are generally considered solitary creatures. They rarely engage in social interaction besides mating. (The relationship of a female with her cubs is an obvious exception.) But there are times and places where polar bears gather in large groups and, though infrequently, even show signs of playing.

An abundance of food, for instance a whale carcass, will sometimes draw dozens of bears. A bowhead whale carcass drifting between the pack ice off Norway attracted 56 polar bears. Eskimos tell of beached bowheads on Alaska's mainland that have attracted 30 or more bears.

Seasonal movement patterns may also bring bears together. In the Hudson's Bay region of Canada, the particular pattern of ice-pack melting results in the unusual phenomenon of large numbers of polar bears spending summers on land. Once fall arrives, they gather at points along the coast to wait for the sea ice to form. The most famous of those points is Cape Churchill in Manitoba, where 50 or more polar bears have been counted at a single time along a $1^1/_4$-mile-long sand spit. Churchill's bears are a major attraction, drawing thousands of visitors each year. Both young and mature bears have been seen playing there. Sometimes they roll and wrestle on the ground; at other times they stand and push or slap each other in the shoulders and chest.

No Churchill-like gatherings exist in modern Alaska. But in a government report, Henry Elliot described a remarkable encounter with polar bears on Alaska's St. Matthew Island in August 1874: "[W]e met bears—yea, hundreds of them. . . . Their white forms in the distance always answered to our search, though they ran from our immediate presence with the greatest celerity. . . their paths were broad and well beaten all over the island. We could not have observed less than 250 or 300 of these animals while we were there." By 1900, however, the bears' numbers on St. Matthew had dropped to near zero, apparently because of intense hunting. ◨

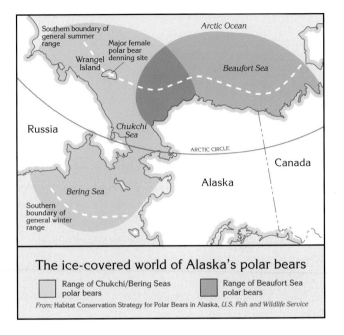

Southern boundary of
general summer
range

Major female
polar bear
denning site

Wrangel
Island

Arctic Ocean

Beaufort Sea

Russia

Chukchi
Sea

ARCTIC CIRCLE

Canada

Bering Sea

Alaska

Southern
boundary of
general winter
range

The ice-covered world of Alaska's polar bears

Range of Chukchi/Bering Seas
polar bears

Range of Beaufort Sea
polar bears

From: Habitat Conservation Strategy for Polar Bears in Alaska, *U.S. Fish and Wildlife Service*

show major east-west movement, Western Alaska bears move
mostly north and south.

Polar bears prefer to remain on sea ice year-round, if possible,
because it's there they find their favorite food: seals. They're most
drawn to sea ice adjacent to mainland coastlines and island arch-
ipelagos, where biological productivity is high and seals are most
abundant. The ice, affected by both ocean currents and winds,
frequently cracks and refreezes. The result is a diverse environment that includes open-water leads and thin ice through which
seals can easily create their breathing holes—the openings
through the ice that give them entry to the sea and a place where
they can surface to breathe.

The open-water leads, long and narrow, may extend for
hundreds of miles and stay open even in subzero cold. They
commonly form where the shifting pack ice and more stable shore-
fast ice meet. Areas of open water that are more rounded and
pond-like also form. Known as polynyas, some are the size of a
football field; others cover hundreds of square miles. Like many

FASCINATING FUR

The polar bear's fur is in two layers: a dense, wool-like underlayer and a more open layer of longer guard hairs.

The hair can take on a number of shades, because the outer guard hairs are not white, but hollow and colorless. The fur looks white largely because of the way it scatters light. A bear that appears white at midday may have a bluish cast to its fur in early morning and then look yellow in the waning light of evening. And if the bear appears darker in high winds, it's because you're seeing glimpses of its black skin as hair is blown aside.

The bear's two-layer fur works well when dry but has little insulating value when wet. What keeps the bear from becoming chilled while swimming in arctic waters is a dense layer of blubber, up to several inches thick.

The hard, hollow guard hairs shed water easily. To dry off, bears need only shake themselves vigorously as they emerge from a swim. These outer hairs have an even more fascinating function: they serve as light tubes that transmit ultraviolet radiation to the skin, where it apparently helps to regulate body heat. ◼

leads, some polynyas survive even the coldest weather. Although they may vary in size from year to year, these recurring polynyas tend to remain in about the same spot and are critically important feeding areas for many marine species, including polar bears.

A DIET OF SEALS

Ringed seals make up the bulk of the polar bear diet. One of the smallest of their kind, ringed seals at maturity average 130 to 150 pounds. Though adults have dark fur, females give birth to

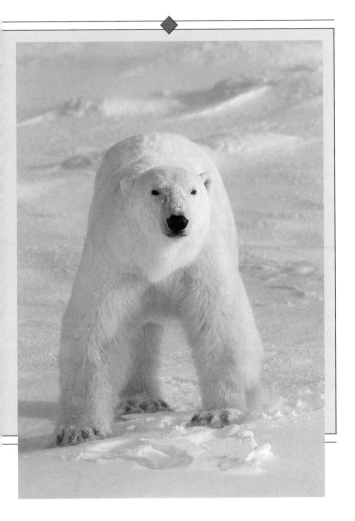

pups with white coats, which camouflage the defenseless young. They are born in April, in snow-covered lairs, or cavities, which incorporate breathing holes in the ice.

Polar bears locate the hidden lairs by smell. While its eyesight and hearing are roughly the same as a human's, a polar bear's sense of smell is extraordinary—enabling it to smell a seal's snow-covered breathing hole from as much as a mile away. (Some people claim polar bears can detect rotting carcasses a hundred miles away.)

Approaching a lair slowly and quietly, the bear apparently places itself directly over the breathing hole and stands absolutely still until it either hears or smells a seal below. Then it raises up on its hind legs and crashes down with its front paws. If the bear breaks through the snow roof on the first try, it grabs for a meal; if not, it may jump on the roof several more times, or dig through it. By then, of course, the seal has usually disappeared through the breathing hole, into the sea.

While polar bears must seek out hidden lairs in winter and early spring, hunting is easier in summer, when breathing holes are exposed and seals can often be found basking on the ice. To catch their prey, the bears have perfected the arts of stalking and still-hunting.

When a bear spots a seal on the ice, it stops and remains motionless, sometimes for several minutes, as if figuring out the best way to get close. Lowering its head, the bear then walks slowly and steadily toward the seal, sometimes moving into a semi-crouched position as it gets close. When it's within 50 to 100 feet, the bear charges, while the stunned seal tries to escape through its hole into the sea.

Though stalks are more dramatic, polar bears more often use still-hunting techniques. They position themselves beside a breathing hole or on the edge of an open-water lead and wait for a seal to surface. They usually lie on their stomach and chest, though some bears prefer to sit or stand. It's essential the bear make no noise because sound is easily transmitted through snow-covered ice. When a seal finally surfaces to breathe, the bear pounces. Biting it on the head or upper body, the bear flips the seal onto the ice; it then bites the seal's head and neck a few more times and drags it several yards from the water before eating it.

The bear first devours the skin and blubber; then, if still hungry, it may eat some meat. The preference is understandable: most of

THE WALRUS CONNECTION

Adult male walrus—weighing up to two tons and wielding long ivory tusks—are among the few animals capable of killing mature polar bears. Yet polar bears will sometimes risk injury to prey on walrus young or, more rarely, adults.

In *Wild Life Beyond the North*, author Frank Illingworth recounts a polar bear–walrus battle described by an earlier arctic explorer: "The bear crept forward with the utmost care, making for the smallest of three animals lying at the edge of the water close under the sleepy eyes of an old bull. As the bear made its final sally the bull turned to the defence of its smaller companion. . . . in a matter of seconds the bear lay bleeding from a mortal wound and the old bull, roaring angrily, lifted itself on its foreflippers and surveyed the scene of its victory before taking to the water."

Anthropologist Richard Nelson was told by Kavik, an Eskimo hunter in Wainwright, Alaska, of a polar bear that tried to get a baby walrus from a herd. "Kavik said that they saw the bear pick up a chunk (or several chunks) of ice with both paws, stand up on its hind legs and throw it at the walruses in a vain attempt to move the large ones away from the infant." ■

the calories are in the blubber, and a polar bear is able to assimilate 97 percent of the fat it ingests.

Polar bears miss their prey far more often than they kill it, averaging about one seal every four or five days. Thus they've had to adapt to a feast-or-famine diet—and a life of constant hunting. They also eat other foods when circumstances allow. They've been seen preying on other seals, beluga whales, walrus, musk oxen, hares, lemmings, ground squirrels, waterfowl, fish, crabs, clams—even, on rare occasions, other polar bears. They also scavenge the carcasses of whales and other marine mammals. And when meat isn't readily available, they've been known to eat bird eggs, kelp, grasses, and berries.

MOTHERS AND THEIR DENS

Unlike Alaska's brown and black bears, most polar bears do not spend their winters in hibernation, because ringed seals provide a reliable year-round supply of food. While any polar bear may build a temporary den to escape extreme cold or arctic storms—when wind-chill temperatures can drop below –100°F—scientists tell us that only pregnant females normally den for extended periods, though some Eskimos disagree with this view.

In Alaska, female polar bears normally begin breeding in their fifth year, mating on the sea ice in April or May over a period of several days after they've been tracked and courted by males. Like brown and black bears, the female polar bears don't release eggs for fertilization until stimulated by the physical act of mating. Impregnated females begin storing fat to get themselves and their cubs-to-be through the next winter; by some estimates, they must gain at least 200 pounds before entering their dens. In one extreme case, a female captured in Canada increased her weight from 214 to 1,112 pounds over a nine-month period.

In most arctic regions, female bears leave the sea ice and come ashore to den between September and November. Most choose sites within 10 miles of the coast, but some have been found 75 miles inland. The females tunnel into snowbanks and build oval chambers. These snow dens are excellent insulators,

Polar bear cubs follow their mom across the ice pack.

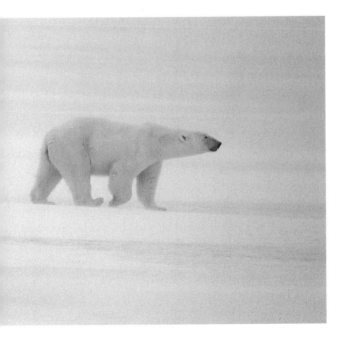

WHEN POLAR BEARS AND HUMANS MEET

Because they are the Arctic's foremost predators, polar bears always prompt discussion of the dangers they pose to humans. Polar bears, it is commonly asserted, are the only bears that regularly stalk people and treat them as prey. Most Eskimo communities in northwestern Alaska will kill or drive away a polar bear that approaches too closely, because it's considered dangerous. Yet while living with the Inupiat Eskimos, anthropologist Richard Nelson was told by hunters that "a bear will usually run away if it sees a man."

While there are many accounts of polar bears stalking people, biologists believe their approach is often triggered by simple curiosity. Another fact to consider: a human is about the same size as a ringed seal. Polar bears, in at least some instances, may mistake a human for a seal. One way that Eskimos have traditionally hunted polar bears is to "play seal," hoping the animal will stalk them.

An analysis of polar bear attacks in Canada between 1965 and 1985 suggests that the adult males stalked humans much as they would a seal.

with the difference between inside and outside temperatures as much as 60°F.

Though they can den wherever there are snowdrifts, pregnant females often concentrate in certain core areas. Such maternity denning areas have been identified in Canada, Greenland, Norway, and Russia. One of the most famous is Wrangel Island, a mountainous, 60-mile-long landform off Russia's northeastern coast. Hundreds of females den here annually, including up to 80 percent of Western Alaska's breeding population.

Farther to the east, Alaska's Beaufort Sea population has proven to be exceptional in that many female bears build dens on sea ice instead of land. Of 90 maternity dens found by polar bear

In nearly every case, the bear had to be killed to end the assault. Often thin or old, some were likely starving animals; others may have been adolescent males that hadn't fine-tuned their hunting skills. Females that assaulted humans usually had cubs and in most cases called off the attack themselves, which suggests they were behaving defensively.

Despite the polar bear's reputation as a dangerous animal, documented accounts of their assaults on people are rare. In Alaska, polar bear biologists and managers have verified only two fatal attacks this century.

The bottom line, according to researcher Steve Amstrup: "Polar bears must be respected because of their size, speed, and strength. When in the bear's world, humans must take extreme care to stay out of their way."

The truth, of course, is that humans have been much more deadly to bears than the other way around. One researcher estimated our species has killed more than 100,000 polar bears since the start of the 18th century. ◨

researcher Steve Amstrup between 1981 and 1991, more than half were on sea ice, some as far as 500 miles offshore—a startling discovery because it had always been assumed that polar bears den exclusively on land, where they escape the danger of having a den crushed, flooded, or broken apart by shifting sea ice.

Amstrup suspects that land dens were more common until the early 1900s, when increased hunting with firearms by Eskimos and whalers killed off the land-denning females or greatly reduced their numbers. In recent years, Alaska's Eskimos have voluntarily decreased their kill of female bears, which may account for a resurgence of maternity land denning along the Beaufort Sea. One preferred area is the Arctic National Wildlife Refuge's coastal plain,

HIDE AND SEEK

One of the most intriguing stories about polar bears is that they cover their black nose when hunting seals. Some arctic explorers and Eskimos say they've seen polar bears use their tongue or paws to hide their nose when stalking their next meal. Some say the bear might even push a chunk of ice ahead of its nose or pack snow around it to conceal the only part of its body not camouflaged by white fur. Polar bear biologists don't completely discredit this legendary behavior, though most remain skeptical. ◼

a political battleground between people who would like to preserve it as wilderness and others who want it opened to oil and gas development.

Settled in their dens, hibernating females give birth in December or January, usually to a pair of cubs. The newborns weigh 1 to 1½ pounds, have such fine hair that they may appear hairless, and are blind. The mother nurses her young on cream-like milk that is 46 percent fat, with more than three times the energy content of either human's or cow's milk, so the young grow quickly. When they emerge from dens in March or April, the cubs weigh 25 to 30 pounds; by their first birthday, they'll weigh up to 200 pounds.

The young bears will stay with Mom for about 28 months as they learn how to hunt seals and survive on the sea ice. Between 20 and 40 percent die their first year; some are killed by other polar bears, but this is considered rare. They are much more likely to starve, be killed by humans, or freeze to death. The hardest times, however, are those first few years after weaning, when bears must adapt to life on their own, and adolescents suffer the highest mortality.

Unless all of a female's cubs die before weaning, at least three years will pass between litters. Given that few polar bears live beyond 20 years in the wild, most females have five litters or less in their lifetime.

FUTURE OF THE POLAR BEAR

Indigenous peoples have hunted polar bears for as long as the two have shared the Arctic. Yet in hunting and killing *nanuq*, they traditionally treated the ice bear with great respect: there were strict rules of conduct to be followed when hunting the bear and after its death. The polar bear was killed not only for its fur and meat, but also as a rite of initiation, to test the courage of boys making the passage to manhood.

An ally of Eskimo shamans, the polar bear was believed to have a powerful spirit. It played a central role in many religious ceremonies, creation legends, and other myths. Some of the rituals are still practiced, stories are still told. But in an era when firearms and snow machines have replaced lances and dog teams, the polar bear has lost much of its power and place of reverence among Eskimo peoples.

A female polar bear with cubs searches for scents on the ice.

European-American explorers, fur traders, whalers, and sport hunters commonly showed polar bears little or none of the respect given by Eskimos. Early visitors to the Arctic often killed any polar bears they saw. In Canada's Amundsen Gulf in 1896, a whaling captain shot 35 polar bears for sport in a single afternoon. Explorer and author Vilhjalmur Stefansson displayed the casual, almost indifferent, attitude that led to the slaughter of polar bears: "I have killed many dozens of polar bears. . . . the risk to men in hunting them is commonly overrated."

The nature of the hunt changed dramatically in the 1940s with the use of ski planes. Trophy hunters from around the world hired planes to fly them across the ice pack, looking for bears. Pilots would often work in tandem: when a polar bear was spotted, one would drop a hunter on the ice while the other herded the bear within shooting range. Worldwide, the reported annual kill in the mid-1960s was 1,300 animals.

Concern over the polar bear slaughter led to a 1965 international meeting of the United States, Canada, Greenland, Norway, and the Soviet Union, resulting in a 1973 agreement that sets limits on the killing and capturing of polar bears and instructs each country to protect polar bear ecosystems. The United States went on to prohibit all hunting of polar bears except for Native subsistence, specifically banning aerial hunting—but giving no special protection to bears in dens or to females with cubs. In 1988 a landmark agreement signed by the Inupiat of Alaska's North Slope and by northwestern Canada's Inuvialuit people included a voluntary limit on their kill of females and cubs in the Beaufort Sea region.

For now, Alaska's polar bear population is considered to be healthy and stable, perhaps even slightly increasing. But the bears remain vulnerable because of the species' low reproduction rate and the relatively small number of bears even when the population is stable.

Overhunting may still be the biggest immediate threat to polar bears throughout the Arctic, especially in areas of heavy poaching, such as parts of Russia. But habitat protection is a growing concern as the Arctic becomes more industrialized, presenting dangers such as oil spills, pesticide contamination, increased human traffic, and disturbance of critical denning and feeding areas.

The United States is the only arctic nation that has not set aside some sort of polar bear sanctuary. The coastal plain of the Arctic National Wildlife Refuge has been serving that purpose, but it never was officially protected as wilderness, and Congress could still open it to development.

One thing seems certain: the polar bear's fate is tied to our species' use of arctic lands and waters and to our willingness to leave vast areas of the circumpolar region in a pristine state for *pisugtooq* ("the great traveler"). ◼

THE BROWN BEAR / GRIZZLY BEAR

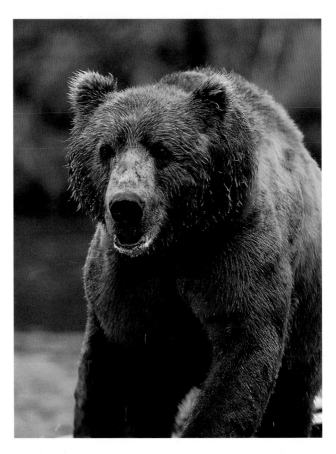

A large male Kodiak bear has a scarred nose from fighting. Kodiak Island is home to North America's largest brown bears.

One North American animal, above all others, has come to symbolize wilderness and raw animal power: the brown bear, also known as the grizzly. This is an animal that requires large, undeveloped landscapes. It is also one that commands our respect when we travel through its ever-shrinking world.

In the distant past, the brown bear's world was a vast one. These bears once roamed through most of Europe and Asia and even occupied a slice of northern Africa. The earliest brown bear fossils, found in China, have been dated at 500,000 years old, and the species itself may go back a million or more years.

The ancestors of modern brown bears apparently migrated from northeast Asia to Alaska along the same Bering Land Bridge taken by the ancestors of Native Americans during the Pleistocene ice age. The bears came in two or more distinct pulses, between 50,000 and 10,000 years ago, and spread throughout much of North America. They once ranged from Northern Alaska and Western Canada south to Mexico, and from the West Coast east across the Great Plains of the United States.

As recently as 1850, an estimated 50,000 to 100,000 brown/grizzly bears inhabited the Lower 48 states. But their range receded and their numbers rapidly declined as they came in contact—and conflict—with European and American explorers and developers. Now fewer than 1,000 remain in the Lower 48. To the north, Canada is home to some 15,000 to 20,000 members of the species *Ursus arctos*. But the great bear's primary North American enclave is Alaska, where an estimated 31,000 live.

The bears occupy nearly the entire state, except for part of the Yukon–Kuskokwim Delta and numerous islands. They inhabit almost every northern ecosystem imaginable, from coastal rain forests to Interior woodlands, high alpine meadows, and arctic tundra. It's no wonder that Alaska is often called the last stronghold of North America's brown bears: this is where they've been given their last, best chance to survive. And even thrive.

As its historic range shows, the brown bear is a remarkably adaptable creature. What especially set it apart from other bears was the species' ability to adapt to the immense open landscapes left by glaciation. Over time, the brown bear developed the tools necessary for tundra life: long claws and powerful neck and back muscles to make it easier to dig plant roots and rodents from the earth, with a large body and aggressive nature to help the bear defend itself—and a female defend its young—in open spaces.

Bears, like humans, can comfortably stand on their hind feet.

Brown bears and grizzlies are essentially the same animal, although the larger, coastal members of *Ursus arctos* are usually referred to as brown bears while the smaller bears of Interior Alaska are called grizzlies. Whether they are labeled browns or grizzlies, the bears have a distinctive body shape characterized by a large shoulder hump, unusually long claws, and a wide, massive head that is concave in profile and frequently described as dish-faced. The body has variously been termed chunky, massive, or sturdy, but browns and grizzlies are anything but clumsy. Or slow. They've been clocked at speeds of up to 40 miles per hour over short distances—fast enough to catch a horse.

Their fur comes in many colors: brown, cinnamon, red, blond, and even black, or a blend of various shades. Many Interior residents have hairs with silvery or frosted tips, which gives their fur a grizzled appearance—hence the name.

Like humans, browns and grizzlies (and other bears) can comfortably stand on two feet. They sometimes do this to see or smell better, feed, engage in play, or fight. But it is not a sign that they're about to attack, as commonly portrayed on magazine covers. Also contrary to popular belief, younger members of the species are excellent climbers, and even adults can pull themselves several yards up a tree if the branches are sturdy enough.

As with many mammals, females tend to live longer than males. Biologists have documented females 30 and older, though a sow in her early to mid-20s is an old bear. Males rarely reach their 20s; one possible reason is that males are frequently injured in fights during the mating season, and over the years these injuries take their toll.

Like other bears, browns and grizzlies have excellent hearing and a superior sense of smell. And their eyesight is quite good, despite the common belief that they have poor vision. The species is considered highly intelligent, in the sense that the bears are able to adapt to a wide range of circumstances and seem capable of "thinking through" problems—for instance, how to reach human food that's been cached in a tree.

SURVIVING WINTER

Among the most fascinating of bear adaptations is winter denning, a strategy that enables the animal to survive prolonged periods of harsh weather and reduced food. Over the millennia,

NATIVE RESPECT

Indigenous peoples have traditionally regarded the brown bear with a mixture of fear and respect. In *The Sacred Paw*, authors Paul Shephard and Barry Sanders write, "From time far older than memory, the bear has been a special being: humanlike, yet close to the animals and hence to the source of life." Native tribes throughout North America traditionally believed the grizzly to be half human, or that humans were descended from bears.

The Koyukon residents of Huslia and Hughes, for example, show an "unparalleled feeling of awe toward brown bears," reports anthropologist Richard Nelson, who lived for several years in those northern Alaska Interior villages. Traditionally when Koyukon men hunted, they followed prescribed rituals. Never should a man brag about hunting a brown bear. And if one is killed, its meat is to be left outside the village for a time, to allow the animal's spiritual energy to depart. The meat is finally shared in a ritual feast that honors the bear's spirit.

Alaska's other Native peoples have historically exhibited similar attitudes. Alutiiq residents of the Alaska Peninsula believed that bears are human ancestors that must be shown respect. Boys being initiated into the hunt would cleanse themselves the night before by taking a sweat bath while an elder chanted. Upon killing his first brown bear, a boy was to put his hand down its throat to remove his fear of the bear and become strong. The hunt would culminate with a ceremonial feast, with bones returned to the kill site, again as a sign of respect.

Traditions are now being forgotten or ignored. As one hunter told anthropologists Jim Fall and Lisa Hutchinson: "The way I was brought up, we got to respect the bear. But nowadays, it's starting to change. They [some other hunters] don't care what happens to the bear after it's dead. . . . But me and my brothers still do the things to the animals that we were taught to do. I don't see no other way." ◼

denning has proved to be a great way for northern bears to spend the winter.

The time at which brown bears enter and leave their dens varies considerably throughout Alaska, but certain generalities apply. Pregnant females are the first to den and, accompanied by newborn cubs, the last to leave their winter shelters, while adult males are the last to den and first to emerge.

At one end of the denning spectrum is Kodiak Island, where adult males may not hibernate at all if the winter weather is relatively mild, snow is scarce, and food can be found. While Kodiak's males vary their winter pattern, pregnant females—more dependent on the security of den sites—are more predictable. They usually enter dens by early November and stay there until late May or even June.

At the other extreme is Alaska's Arctic, where pregnant females spend up to eight months in dens, from mid-September to late May. Males more typically enter dens in mid-October and leave by mid-May.

In the coldest regions, where midwinter temperatures may fall to -60°F, the bears often choose sites where snow builds up, adding insulation for the dens beneath the ground. The timing of denning in these regions may be tied to the season's first heavy snowfall.

Browns and grizzlies most commonly dig their own dens in the earth, usually on moderate to steep slopes. A den is often prepared weeks before the bear goes into hibernation. The underground shelters are built to size for the most efficient use of body heat and may consist of both an entry tunnel and a denning chamber. Some bears add nests of grass, willow, or whatever plants are available.

Alaska Range grizzlies usually dig fairly shallow dens, with roofs six inches to a foot thick. Facing almost any direction, they are built at a wide range of elevations, from riverbanks to high mountain slopes. Frequently they're dug among clumps of willows, perhaps for the stability that roots provide.

In Southeast Alaska, meanwhile, brown bears prefer old-growth forest; sites are commonly excavated under live trees or

OF BROWNS AND GRIZZLIES

Above, an Interior grizzly bear feeds on tundra blueberries;
right, a McNeil River brown bear catches a salmon.

What, exactly, is the difference between a brown bear and a grizzly bear? The distinction, it turns out, is a rather arbitrary one for these animals that all belong to the species *Ursus arctos*. In general terms, brown bears are coastal animals, while members of the same species living in interior regions are known as grizzlies. The grizzlies tend to have longer claws and a bigger hump, be lighter in color, and have a more dish-shaped face than their coastal cousins. On average, they are also considerably smaller, mainly because brown bears have access to more plentiful energy-rich foods, especially salmon.

Adult female grizzlies on the North Slope average about 220 pounds in springtime, while those in the Alaska Range average closer to 280. By fall, adult bears often weigh up to $1\frac{1}{2}$ times as much as they did only four months earlier, so an adult female that weighs

260 pounds in May may tip the scales at 400 by the time it enters its winter den. A large male grizzly may weigh 400 to 500 pounds in spring and 600 to 700 just before denning.

And brown bears? Adult females average 400 to 500 pounds in early summer, sometimes reaching 600 to 700 in fall. Males, meanwhile, range from 500 to 900 pounds, with some giants reaching autumn weights of 1,500 pounds or more.

Coastal browns live in denser populations than grizzlies, again reflecting habitat and food differences. Kodiak and Admiralty Islands and the Katmai region of the Alaska Peninsula average about one bear per square mile. At the other extreme is the eastern Brooks Range, which can sustain only one grizzly for every 35 to 40 square miles.

Home ranges—the areas that meet all of an individual bear's requirements for food, shelter, mating, and denning—show similar variability. On Admiralty Island, for example, females have ranges that average 10 square miles, while on the North Slope they average 130 square miles. Males' home ranges are typically two to four times larger. ◼

snags. Though dirt dens are preferred throughout most of Alaska, brown bears often use natural rock cavities on both Kodiak and Admiralty Islands, where milder winters make snow insulation less important.

Inside the den, bears enter a state of hibernation in which body temperatures and metabolic functions are only slightly reduced. They don't eat, drink, defecate, or urinate throughout their dormancy, and survive by living off fat reserves.

LIFE AS A CUB

All of Alaska's brown and grizzly bears begin their lives in January or February, within protected dens. Pregnant females give birth to litters of one to four cubs, most commonly two. Blind, toothless, nearly naked, and helpless, the newborns weigh a pound or less, small enough to fit into a human's cupped hands. The cubs begin nursing almost immediately and, nourished by rich milk, grow quickly.

Upon leaving their den in spring, cubs weigh about 15 pounds; by autumn they may weigh 60 to 70 pounds. Because their young are highly vulnerable, females with newborn cubs usually spend their first weeks in out-of-the-way, protected places with good visibility, such as upper ridges.

Like other members of the species, a new mother emerging from her den goes through a transitional "walking hibernation" phase, characterized by lethargy and poor appetite, as she internally shifts gears from wintertime torpor to a highly active summertime mode. While it takes several days for Mom to work up an appetite, first-year cubs have frequent hunger pains and nurse every two to three hours.

Being new to the world and its myriad hazards, first-year cubs are absolutely dependent on Mom. Exactly how they key in to her isn't clear. New cubs don't seem to have a well-developed sense of smell, so visual and auditory signals may be more crucial to their

Brown bear cubs nurse; the milk they drink is rich in fat.

bonding process. For instance, females may use distress calls, such as a woofing sound, when separated from their cubs.

A separation between mother and young can, in rare instances, lead to temporary cub adoption. Such adoptions have been observed at Alaska's McNeil River State Game Sanctuary, where dozens of brown bears congregate each summer to feed on salmon. Cubs that become separated from their mother occasionally join up with other family groups. The adoptions are usually brief, lasting from a few minutes to several hours. But in one case, a cub remained with its new family an entire season.

Adult bears pose the greatest threat to brown and grizzly cubs. The usual mortality rate for first-year cubs is between 30 and

40 percent, and most are killed (and sometimes eaten) by other brown/grizzly bears. The general consensus until recently was that only adult males kill cubs, but adult females have been seen killing cubs that belong to another family.

Cubs also face the danger of death from disease, malnutrition, and accidents like falls and drownings. Larger litters often have runts unable to compete with the rest; some die right in the den.

Cubs that survive their first year have a good chance of reaching adulthood, because mortality rates drop sharply after the first year. The next major hurdle follows weaning, when adolescents are driven away to fend for themselves. Young brown bears are generally weaned during their third spring, at age $2^1/_2$. It appears there's a hormonal shift in the female related to the end of lactation, and she simply stops being a mom.

Larry Aumiller, longtime manager of the McNeil sanctuary, once watched as a female turned on her pair of $2^1/_2$-year-old cubs. "All of a sudden, she lunged at them," he recalls. "They were really befuddled." Over the next two days, the female became increasingly aggressive, chasing the cubs and even biting them on the rump until they left. In less than a week, she went into estrus and mated.

Weaned siblings may remain together for a season or two, sometimes even denning together. But as they approach maturity, they inevitably part. Females tend to establish home ranges that overlap, or are adjacent to, their mother's. Males, however, are likely to wander far in search of new stomping grounds.

OPPORTUNISTIC OMNIVORES

Descended from carnivores, brown bears have evolved into opportunistic omnivores. John Muir once commented: "To him almost everything is food except granite." An exaggeration, but not far off the mark. The species eats an extremely wide variety of

CLASSIFYING THE BROWNS

Because they vary so much in physical appearance, brown/grizzly bears were once classified into hundreds of subspecies. In 1918, scientist C. H. Merriam identified more than 90 subspecies in North America alone. In 1963, biologist Bob Rausch offered the simplified classification generally accepted today: that all North American brown/grizzly bears belong to a single subspecies, *Ursus arctos horribilis*, with the exception of Kodiak Island browns, recognized as *Ursus arctos middendorffi*.

The skulls of Kodiak bears tend to be wider, a little more massive, reflecting thousands of years of isolation from mainland populations. The Kodiak Archipelago was likely first populated with brown bears during one of the Pleistocene's glacial periods, when bears may have crossed an ice bridge to the island or perhaps ridden across Shelikof Strait on ice floes. However they got there, Kodiak's browns evolved into the continent's largest: males may weigh up to 1,500 or 1,600 pounds in fall.

Recent genetic work by Gerry Shields and Sandra Talbot has raised questions about these subspecies distinctions. Their studies at the University of Alaska's Institute of Arctic Biology show that Kodiak and mainland bears are similar enough genetically to be classified as the same subspecies. What's more, those studies reveal that brown bears on Southeast Alaska's Admiralty, Baranof, and Chichagof Islands—the ABC bears—are genetically distinct from all other Alaskan brown bears. Most intriguing of all, the research suggests that the ABC bears are genetically more closely linked to polar bears than to other brown bears. ◾

foods: everything from insects and berries to fish, carrion, and human garbage.

Bears consume enormous quantities of grass and sedges at certain times of year, but they also show a taste for meat when available. Biologist Sterling Miller, who has studied grizzly predation on moose, says, "For the first couple weeks after calves are born, grizzlies can kill them with impunity." But calves remain highly vulnerable for only a short period: three to four weeks for moose and two to three weeks for caribou. After that, bear predation drops dramatically. The adult hooved animals that are occasionally killed by grizzlies are usually sick, injured, or old.

In only one sense are browns and grizzlies picky eaters: they prefer the high-energy, high-protein food sources needed to build fat reserves for their long winter dormancy. And they need large quantities of it. Adult bears may consume up to 80 or 90 pounds of food per day during their feeding peak in late summer and autumn, adding 3 to 6 pounds of fat daily.

Because the best foods vary by both season and location, bears must be in the right place at the right time to take advantage of them. Within each of Alaska's major regions, they follow predictable feeding patterns as spring gives way to summer and then fall.

On Kodiak Island, for example, browns initially focus on vegetation. Many graze on sedges and other herbaceous plants found in alpine meadows. Others descend to intertidal beaches to feed on newly emergent plants or the "beach lice" (tiny saltwater organisms) found in kelp beds. Springtime plants are supplemented, when possible, by the bodies of deer that died during the winter or by newborn fawns.

By late June, salmon begin entering Kodiak's streams, and most bears migrate to favorite fishing sites. A few, however, stay in alpine areas, continuing to graze on plants. As berry crops ripen in mid-August, many bears shift to a diet of elderberries and salmonberries. Others mix fish and berries. Fall presents a mixed bag of berries, salmon, roots, and rodents (voles are a favorite) as bears gorge themselves for hibernation.

At the other extreme are the grizzlies of the Arctic. When they first leave their dens, there's little to eat besides overwintered berries or the remains of mammals that died in winter. Green-up

The claws of grizzly and brown bears are ideal for digging.

finally begins in June, and from then through July the bears depend mostly on succulent vegetation such as sedges and Richardson's saxifrage, supplemented by the roots of pea-family plants and a variety of rodents: ground squirrels, mice, voles, and lemmings. Caribou calves and, less commonly, adults are

49

occasionally preyed on but are not a critical ingredient in most arctic bears' diets. Berries, roots, tubers, and rodents are important foods from August into fall, with ground squirrels an especially critical source of calories.

SOCIAL LIFE

Brown/grizzly bears were long considered to be solitary creatures, living in isolation from each other except during the mating season. But that simplistic notion has changed.

Females, for example, spend much of their life in family units, with a succession of offspring. Siblings may spend one or more seasons in each other's company after weaning. Cubs, adolescents, and even occasional adults demonstrate play behavior. And dozens of individuals sometimes gather in close quarters to feed. Both males and females breed with several partners over the course of a lifetime or even a single season, and such coupled bears may remain together anywhere from a few days to a week or more, when they'll eat, sleep, and travel together.

Based on his many years at the McNeil sanctuary, Larry Aumiller is convinced almost any bear will play: "I've even seen 20-plus-year-old males playing, though that's pretty rare. And I've seen a female with spring cubs [temporarily] abandon its cubs to go off and play with an old buddy." Females also will play with their cubs. Among bears' play activities: wrestling, playing tag, chasing each other in circles, playing with sticks or rocks, sliding down snowbanks.

Social interactions are most obvious within families. But even adult males, which lead a more unsociable lifestyle, share their overlapping ranges with other bears and participate in group feeds at salmon streams, beached whales, berry patches, or garbage dumps.

When brown bears congregate, a social hierarchy inevitably develops, with dominance based largely on size. Even the biggest

Brown bear cubs playing.

males, however, tend to avoid confrontations with females who have cubs. The females often show great ferocity in protecting their offspring. Some will fight to the death if necessary. This combativeness may have been an adaptation to life in wide-open spaces during the ice ages, with natural selection favoring females that effectively defended their families in a treeless environment.

Because the personal space of individual bears is inevitably invaded in groups, tension often builds, with stress signaled in a number of ways: yawning, heavy salivation, laid-back ears, body posture, vocalizations (such as growls or huffing), and deliberate movements. Yet only rarely do encounters between stressed-out bears result in fights; less dominant bears are usually given an opportunity to back away. Slowly.

A grizzly scratches its back against a signpost in Denali Park.

FUTURE OF THE BROWN BEAR

The settlers and developers of the United States nearly wiped out the brown bear in the Lower 48, killing the animal whenever possible and destroying its habitat. In Alaska, the great bear has been luckier. Large expanses have been set aside in parks, preserves, refuges, and forests, giving it the space and solitude it needs. Because of the brown bear's demands for space and food, it is sometimes considered an indicator species, one whose well-being serves as a measure of an ecosystem's health.

The state's population of brown/grizzly bears seems secure for now, but the species does face threats. One is human population growth in areas occupied by bears, which inevitably leads to people killing bears that appear to be threatening them or their property. In Southcentral Alaska's Nelchina Basin, homesteaders now report

THE WAY HOME

Because they live in overlapping ranges, Alaska's brown bears are not considered territorial creatures in the manner of wolves. Yet they do show strong attachments to place when forcibly removed from familiar grounds, and some individuals have demonstrated a remarkable ability to find the way home. One young male in Prince William Sound gave a spectacular demonstration of homing instincts. Transplanted from Cordova, where it had become a nuisance, the bear was taken to Montague Island, more than 40 air miles away. Less than a month later, it had returned to the Cordova dump. To do so, it had to swim a minimum of 5 miles across open water with strong tidal currents.

WHEN GRIZZLIES AND HUMANS MEET

The great size and strength of the brown/grizzly bear, its fierce nature when protecting its young or its food, and the fact that it's a carnivore equipped to kill other large mammals have made it a frightening creature to our species. Many people still believe in the simplistic and inaccurate myth of the grizzly as a bloodthirsty animal that lurks in the shadows, waiting to attack anything that crosses its path, humans included.

The truth is that brown/grizzly bears as a rule are wary of humans and avoid them when possible, except when they've learned to associate people with food. They are much more likely to flee from humans than to approach them. The species as a whole is not a predator of humans, and deaths from maulings are rare (a total of 21 people in Alaska this century). Most human injuries and deaths result from sudden, close encounters in which the bear is surprised and feels threatened. Once the threat is removed, the attack ends, which is why people are told to "play dead" if attacked.

As with other bears, the fact is that we present a much greater threat to them than they do to us. Each year, hundreds are killed in Alaska by trophy hunters, subsistence users, and people who feel threatened.

Bear-viewing programs are helping to reshape our knowledge of brown/grizzly bears and our attitudes toward them. At public viewing places in Alaska, the bears have shown they will adapt to, and tolerate, a human presence without harm to either species. The key is that these bears have become habituated to people, but don't associate us with food. Larry Aumiller, of the McNeil River State Game Sanctuary, says that "over time it's become clear from their actions that the more tolerant bears perceive us as neutral objects, maybe as innocuous as a rock or a tree." The intolerant ones, meanwhile, leave when humans arrive.

A critical ingredient of safe bear-human interactions is respect for the animal and its great power, and knowledge of its behaviors. By knowing about the bear, we can minimize harmful encounters. ◼

Brown bear cubs usually stay with their mom until age 2 ¹/₂.

"bear problems," because they've moved into grizzly territory. And they want fewer bears.

A bigger threat comes from resource activities like mining and logging that can endanger bear habitat. The big fear is the cumulative effect of long-term, incremental loss of land the bears depend on. In Southeast Alaska, some bear lands are being compromised by logging and associated road-building. On the North Slope, oil and gas projects could eventually fragment the habitat.

Land and wildlife managers need to do long-range planning. Five-year or ten-year plans aren't enough; we need to be thinking at least a century ahead. ■

TIPS FOR TRAVELING IN BEAR COUNTRY

An aspect of bear behavior that merits special discussion is the animal's alleged unpredictability. Bear specialist Larry Aumiller says the question of whether a bear that encounters a human will charge or flee is predictable "to a certain degree . . . but it requires an understanding of bear behavior. Just like a human, a bear's response depends on many factors: How close are you? What's your behavior? Does the bear have cubs?" But also like humans, bears have differing temperaments—some might be called easygoing; others are more excitable. Different bears are likely to respond with different intensity to perceived threats.

Still, Aumiller stresses, "For the most part, bears are perfectly predictable. For example, a little bear is going to defer to a big bear. And bears will respond to a food source, whether it's salmon or garbage. In the extreme, if you believe that a bear's behavior is totally unpredictable, a result of random choice, then it doesn't really matter what you do in bear country. But that's not the case. There are, in fact, certain precautions, certain actions a person can take to avoid a confrontation, based on what we do know of bears' behavior."

Below are tips for going through bear country:

While hiking or camping:

■ Avoid sudden encounters. Most attacks occur when a bear is surprised or feels threatened. Whenever possible, travel in open country, during daylight hours, and in groups. Make noise when passing through forested areas or thick brush. Talking or singing is preferable to using "bear bells." Leave the family dog at home; dogs can provoke encounters.

■ Keep alert. Look for signs of bear, such as fresh tracks, scat, matted vegetation, or partly eaten salmon.

■ Choose your tent site carefully. Pitch the tent well away from trails, streams with spawning salmon, and berry patches. Avoid areas where scavengers have gathered or which have a rotten smell. Bears will often aggressively defend their food supplies.

■ Beware of attracting bears with your food. Cook meals at least 100 feet from tents. Store food away from campsites, hung high between trees whenever possible or placed in bear-resistant containers (see photo). If you've been fishing, change your clothes before entering your tent, and store them away from camp. Avoid odorous foods, and wash up after cooking and eating. Store garbage in an airtight container or burn it, and pack out the remains.

■ Carry a gun only if you know how to use it. One alternative is red-pepper spray, which comes in aerosol cans. Because the canisters sometimes leak, it's best to store bear sprays in airtight containers. (Notify pilots that you are carrying bear sprays; a leakage could disable a pilot and lead to a crash.)

If you encounter a bear:

■ Talk to the bear, to identify yourself as a human. Talk, but don't yell. And don't run. Running from a bear is usually the worst possible action because it will trigger a bear's predatory instincts, and a bear can easily outrun you. Back away slowly, and give the bear an escape route. Avoid getting between a mother and her cubs.

■ Increase your apparent size. Raise your arms above your head in order to appear larger, and wave your arms slowly to better identify yourself as human. As a rule, bigger is better with bears, which are less likely to attack a larger target. With two or more people, it helps to stand side by side. (In a forested area, it might be appropriate to climb a tree, but remember that black bears and young grizzlies can climb.)

■ Play dead if the bear charges and makes contact with you. Fall to the ground, lie flat on your stomach or curl into a ball, hands behind your neck, and remain passive. If you are wearing a pack, leave it on. Once a bear feels there is no longer a threat, the attack will usually end. Wait for the bear to leave before you move. The exception to this rule is when a bear shows predatory behavior. Instead of simply charging, a bear that is actually hunting for prey will show intense interest while approaching at a walk or a run, or by circling, as if stalking you. If you're being treated as prey, fight back. Such circumstances are exceedingly rare and most often involve black bears.

A good summary of bear-safety tips is available in a free brochure titled "*Bear Facts*," published jointly by several state and federal agencies in Alaska. Another excellent resource is Stephen Herrero's book *Bear Attacks: Their Causes and Avoidance.* ■

IS IT A BROWN BEAR

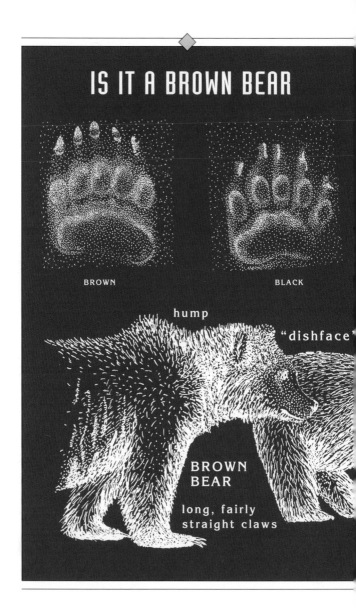

BROWN

BLACK

hump

"dishface"

BROWN
BEAR

long, fairly
straight claws

OR A BLACK BEAR?

Several physical traits distinguish black bears from brown bears (grizzlies). Color, curiously enough, is not necessarily one of them. Most of Alaska's black bears are indeed black, but some are cinnamon or brown and a few are bluish gray. And some brown bears can look closer to black. Neither is size a dependable distinguishing trait, despite the fact that black bears in general are smaller than brown bears.

It's best to look for the prominent characteristics that mark the difference between the two species. The brown bear has a shoulder hump; the black bear doesn't. Brown bears have a somewhat concave, dish-shaped face; blacks have a straighter profile (a Roman nose).

Black bears have shorter, more curved claws than brown bears, resulting in different tracks. The two species also have different toe imprints. The toes of a black bear show more arc and are more separated than those of a brown, which tend to be close together and more in a line. ■

"Roman nose"

BLACK BEAR

short, curved claws

THE BLACK BEAR

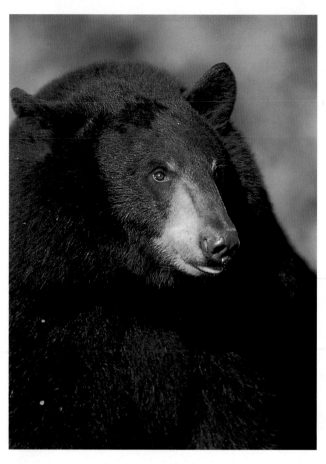

A creature of the forest, the black bear is more secretive and less aggressive than either grizzly or polar bears.

he smallest and most common of Alaska's three bears, *Ursus americanus* may also be the most enigmatic. A creature of forest and shadow, the black bear has followed an evolutionary path that's made it more secretive and less aggressive than the brown bear or polar bear. It moves like a phantom through woods of spruce and hemlock, cottonwood and birch. Yet for all its wariness—or perhaps because of it—the black bear has proved remarkably adaptable to human development and human intolerance.

The black bear doesn't require vast areas of wilderness to thrive. If there's sufficient food and cover for hiding, members of the species seem equally at home in deep, pristine forests or along the wooded edges of Alaska's largest cities. There the black bear remains mostly invisible—until it develops a taste for human food or garbage. Then the phantom may become a nuisance or even a threat—a problem bear, as we humans put it.

More images to consider. *Ursus americanus* is sometimes called the all-American bear, partly because it lives only in North America (another black bear species, *Ursus thibetanus*, inhabits Asia), but also because it's so common, familiar to people across the continent. Biologists estimate that a half million black bears inhabit North America. They range from Canada to northern Mexico (though not everywhere in between) and are found in 40 states. Their homelands include arid Southwest chaparral, eastern swamps, Northwest rain forests, and boreal woodlands.

In Alaska, black bears occupy three-quarters of the state, from the Southeast panhandle to the Brooks Range, though their densities vary greatly, from 10 to 100 animals per 100 square miles, depending on the quality of habitat. The species is absent from unforested mainland regions—the Seward and Alaska Peninsulas, the North Slope, and portions of the Yukon-Kuskokwim Delta—and many islands. When pressed for Alaska's population, some biologists guess 30,000 to 100,000 black bears. Others won't even try. Being a forest animal, the black bear is nearly impossible to census. But on one point, black bear researchers agree: the statewide population is "very healthy."

Here's the irony in all this talk about an all-American bear: for centuries we humans have widely considered the black bear a lesser bruin than its more charismatic relatives. The species' small size and timid nature—at least by ursine standards—account for much of this stereotyping. For some Native peoples, however, the black bear is a being of great spiritual power and an important subsistence species whose meat is a favored delicacy. Others simply delight in the black bear as a wild creature of the woods.

There is also this paradox: almost always, black bears—even moms with cubs—choose flight over fight when surprised or threatened; but on exceedingly rare occasions, for unknown reasons, a black bear will stalk and kill a person.

As it moves through the forest of our human psyches, the black bear seems to be constantly shifting shapes, changing identities. This confuses us and sometimes frightens us, contributes to flawed notions of the bear's nature, lessens our acceptance of what is really a shy, tolerant animal.

A CREATURE OF THE FOREST

Of North America's three modern bears, only the black is a native species. Both the brown and polar bears evolved into their present-day forms while still in Asia, then later migrated here. But the black bear became what it is today while already inhabiting this continent.

By most accounts, the ancestors of present-day black bears moved from Asia to North America 1 to 4 million years ago, across an early version of the Bering Land Bridge later traveled by humans and brown bears. Those early American settlers were shy, smallish, forest-dwelling omnivores belonging to the species *Ursus etruscus.*

Spread across Asia, Europe, and North America, the Etruscan bears eventually split into three distinct lines. But only one, the black bear line, would survive into the present as a creature of the woods. Like its ancestors, the modern Alaskan black bear is a shy, omnivorous animal, with a body and behavior that reflect adaptations to life in the northern forest—and to the presence of a more dominant competitor, the brown bear.

Consider tree climbing. Adult black bears, unlike their grizzly counterparts, are adept tree climbers. The reason, scientists

A black bear crosses a meadow of fireweed on the edge of the forest.

suspect: during its evolution as a forest creature, the black bear found it easier to retreat from danger than to fight. And the escape path it chose was up a tree. To be efficient climbers, black bears maintained a comparatively small body size. And they evolved strong, sharp, narrow, curved claws: good climbing tools.

Because grizzlies prey on black bears where their ranges overlap, the grizzly's arrival in North America may have reinforced the black bear's dependence on forest sanctuaries. More than ever, trees became a refuge critical to its survival.

The black bear's reliance on trees as safe havens is perhaps best shown by the behavior of females defending their cubs. As

Canadian researcher Stephen Herrero writes in *Bear Attacks*, "The mother's response when threatened with potential danger will be to flee with the offspring, to climb a tree with them, or to stay on the ground and direct aggressive actions toward the intruder while the cubs find shelter up a tree or in dense vegetation. . . . Trees or dense brush are the core of the mother bear's defense of offspring." Even when defending their cubs, black bear moms seldom attack. Herrero calls them great bluffers and speculates that they've evolved behaviors to scare off threats without the need of combat.

Females with cubs often seek out the bases of large trees for nursing or sleeping. An Alaskan favorite is the cottonwood, which has deep grooves and is easily climbed. If danger approaches, it's simple for the cubs to scoot up the tree. More rarely, moms will take their young up into a tree for nursing or napping. And sometimes they'll use trees as a kind of baby-sitter, sending their cubs up high while they go off to feed.

Though tree-climbing has evolved as a key survival mechanism, it is also done for recreation and play. Cubs especially like to run up and down trees.

And bears of all ages will climb to reach certain foods. Acorns, beechnuts, hickory nuts, hazelnuts, and pine nuts are favorites in the Lower 48, while Alaska's black bears go for aspen and cottonwood buds.

MAINLY VEGETARIAN

Just as forest life has influenced the black bear's physical characteristics and demeanor, these in turn have affected its feeding habits. Besides the fact that they're generally nonaggressive, blacks are also small bears. In Alaska, adult females usually weigh between 120 and 175 pounds, while males range from 200 to 400 pounds. Adult weights vary greatly throughout the black bear's range, depending on quality of habitat, climate, and food supplies.

A BLACK BEAR CAN BE BLOND

The black bear can be many colors—including brown. Colors range from jet black to chocolate brown, cinnamon, honey, blond, blue, and even white. Even black bears with black coats aren't entirely black: most have brownish muzzles, and many have white to cream-colored V-shaped patches on their chest or throat.

Color variations correlate with habitat and climate. Black is the perfect color for a bear that lives among shadows, like those in moist, densely forested areas. There, the bear itself becomes a shadow in the forest. But earth tones, not shadows, may be more important camouflage in brighter and more open arid regions. In sparsely vegetated areas, lighter coats may help prevent bears from overheating because they don't absorb as much solar heat as black coats.

Thus the large majority of black bears east of the Mississippi River are indeed black, as are those in Minnesota and the Pacific Northwest; those in the southwestern United States, however, are mostly brown to blond. In Alaska, as you would expect, the great majority of black bears are in fact black. Less than 10 percent are cinnamon or brown. A tiny fraction have bluish gray coats; these so-called glacier bears (see photo above) are found only along the Gulf of Alaska coast, between Yakutat and Juneau. Even rarer is the white-furred Kermode bear, or spirit bear, which inhabits islands along the British Columbia coast. ◼

A cinnamon-colored black bear walks across snow.

Alaska's biggest black bears are found on Prince of Wales Island; there, large males may weigh 400 to 500 pounds.

Given their retiring nature and smallish though bulky build, it's not surprising that black bears—despite being classified as carnivores—are omnivorous creatures whose diet is 80 to 90 percent vegetarian. Predatory behavior is therefore rare, with notable exceptions. Studies on Alaska's Kenai Peninsula indicate that black bears kill up to 35 percent of the region's moose calves each spring. They also eat snowshoe hares, mice, voles, birds and their eggs, insects, and carrion. And in some coastal regions, they'll catch salmon in spawning streams.

Because they'll lose one-fourth to one-half of their body weight while hibernating, Alaska's black bears (like brown bears) must build huge fat reserves in only a few months' time. And they must do so on a diet that's largely grasses, sedges, horsetails, insects, and berries. Black bears therefore spend most of their waking hours eating or looking for food. Exceptions, of course, are made during the breeding season.

This doesn't mean black bears consume everything remotely edible; they clearly show a preference for easily digestible and highly nutritional foods. In spring and early summer they seek out young grass shoots and other emerging plants, like horsetails, sedges, wild celery, skunk cabbage, or blue-joint grass. They may also sample catkins, tree buds, overwintered berries, and the roots of some flowers. If carcasses or eggs are available, they'll eat those too, along with ants, wasps, and bees. Still, some bears continue to lose weight until the really heavy eating begins with the arrival of berry season.

Crowberries, huckleberries, cranberries, and blueberries are Alaskan black bear favorites, but devil's club berries seem to be a special treat. Department of Fish and Game researcher Chuck Schwartz says that on the Kenai Peninsula, "I've seen black bears migrate 50 to 70 miles to feed in devil's club patches. It's usually the first abundant producer of fruit and it provides lots of energy. I've tried the berries; they're not palatable to humans, they taste like turpentine. But black bears sure love them." Even when they have access to salmon, black bears may show a preference for the carbohydrate-rich berries, whose sugars are more easily converted to fat.

THE KOYUKON VIEW

Alaska's Native peoples know the black bear (see photo) by many names. Different Athabascan groups call it *sis, ghedisla,* or *shoh zhraii,* while to the Tlingit it is *s'eek,* to Eyaks, *tsiya,* and to Eskimos, *iyyagrig.* Whatever its given name, the species has traditionally been an important part of Native subsistence culture. The bear's meat is an important food, and its fat, rendered into lard, is used for cooking. In some regions, its hide serves as a mattress or blanket. As anthropologist Richard Nelson reports in his book *Make Prayers to the Raven,* the black bear also ranks high among some tribes as a ceremonial delicacy and a spirit being. Among the Koyukon Athabascan of Alaska's northern Interior, says Nelson, it "takes us near the apex of power among spirits of the natural world," below only the grizzly and wolverine.

Nelson's story about the Koyukon people documents the traditional relationship of one Native tribe with the black bear, whom the Koyukon know as *sis.* "Their knowledge of these animals is deep and detailed," he tells us, "their hunting methods sophisticated and complex. . . ." And their respect for the bear's spirit is immense. For that reason the hunt is a quest for prestige as well as food, an expression of manhood. Because its spirit is so potent, "People's behavior toward black bears is subject to an extraordinary number of taboos.

"Disregarding or violating bear taboos can be sharply punished," Nelson writes. "Ordinary offenses alienate the animal, make it elusive or invisible. . . . More serious offenses can bring illness to the person or a family member, or even death. Insulting comments or gestures toward the animal, whether it is dead or alive, rank among the most severe transgressions. Bear attacks, which are exceedingly rare, may be interpreted as retaliation for such insults."

Koyukon women traditionally face the most taboos. They are not to speak the black bear's name, instead calling it *hulzinh* ("dark one") to keep from offending its spirit. They may not hunt bears and should even avoid looking at a black bear.

Hunters, too, must be careful not to offend the bear. When speaking about a denning bear he's found, a man will discuss his discovery using indirect words. Cryptic language is even more important when a bear is killed, because speaking directly about the kill would offend its spirit. A successful hunter might simply remark, "I found something in a hole."

Elaborate rules govern the treatment of a dead bear's remains. If killed in a den, it must be pulled out "the old way," by hand or rope, and then immediately skinned and butchered. The head is removed and hung in a nearby tree or burned, and the hide is handled carefully, because bear skins keep their life force for several years. The use of various internal organs is also governed by rules; for instance, no one should eat the first neck joint, because it causes slowness, as reflected in the way a bear moves its head slowly.

A few days after a bear is killed, men and boys gather for a ceremonial feast, a "bear party." Held in the woods, away from female influence, the feast is "a memorial potlatch held to honor the killed animal."

The final mark of respect is proper disposal of its bones; usually that means burning them in a clean fire. ◘

By late fall, more than half of a bear's body weight will be fat. Once those fat reserves reach a certain level, an internal mechanism shuts off the bear's appetite, and its body chemistry begins adjusting for the long sleep ahead.

INTO THE WINTER DEN

Additional factors, beyond fat reserves, likely influence the time of denning. Food availability is one. Weather conditions and amount of daylight are others. The timing varies from region to region and year to year, but most bears enter their dens by late October or early November and, with few exceptions, they remain there until April or May. As with brown bears, pregnant females den earliest and emerge latest, while adult males have the shortest denning period. On average, Alaska's black bears annually spend 190 to 230 days denned up.

Black bears make their dens in almost every imaginable place. They've been found in hollow trees, caves, brush piles, highway culverts, and even under houses. On the Kenai Peninsula, more than 90 percent are ground excavations on gentle slopes, within upland forest. In other regions of Alaska, however, half or less of the dens that biologists have discovered were excavations.

Fish and Game bear biologist Sterling Miller found one den in a Susitna Valley cliff. The opening was a narrow crack and "you had to crawl in 20 feet before you reached a nice, big nesting chamber." Another bear climbed 30 feet inside a hollow cottonwood; one crawled among a jumble of boulders. Some of the dens have probably been used for centuries (though it's rare for an individual bear to return to the same site in consecutive years) and have thick, comfortable—at least to a bear—mats of grass. At the other extreme are excavated dens that last only a single season.

In the Tanana Flats region near Fairbanks, bear researcher John Hechtel once found three surface nests in a single season.

Though they are mainly vegetarian, black bears will eat salmon.

"Each of the bears had dug a shallow trench, just a few inches deep, and let the snow drift over them," he recalls. "One of them wasn't much more than an ice bubble when I saw it." Those are among the stranger denning choices, given the region's severe and

WHEN BLACK BEARS AND HUMANS MEET

Black bears don't share the reputation of the brown/grizzly bear for ferocity. Over the years, they've injured many more people than brown bears have, but more than 90 percent of those injuries were minor, while injuries from brown bears are usually serious. More notable than the black bear's occasional aggression is its restraint. Given the large population of North American black bears, attacks happen very seldom. Most occur when people feed the bears, tease them, poke them, or even try to pet them or shake hands with them.

Unlike encounters with grizzlies, surprise meetings with black bears—even moms with cubs—rarely lead to injury. Some experts suggest backing away quietly during close encounters, while others recommend mild human aggression: assuming a dominant posture and speaking assertively, in a calm voice, while giving the bear room to escape. In the unlikely case of a mom attacking to defend her cubs, passive resistance—playing dead—is best.

On rare occasions, some black bears appear to treat humans as prey. Stephen Herrero, author of *Bear Attacks*, says predatory behavior is most commonly associated with wild black bears in rural or remote areas, where they have relatively little association with people. In other words, in areas similar to much of Alaska. "A typical predation scenario," Herrero writes, "might involve the bear slowly approaching a person during the day, perhaps partly circling and then rushing toward the person, trying to knock the intended prey down and inflicting injuries. . . . "

A black bear hunting its prey will continue the attack until the prey escapes or dies. Thus if you suspect a black bear considers you its prey, do not play dead. Instead, fight back, hitting the bear in the face—the nose is a prime target—with whatever weapon you have: firearms, an ax, a large piece of wood, a rock. But to put these rare cases of black bear aggression into context, consider this: you're nearly 100,000 times more likely to be killed by another human than by a black bear. ◼

prolonged winters. Another female piled dried grass into a haystack-like mound, then burrowed into it with her three 2-year-old cubs. As in other areas, most of the Tanana Flats bears built insulating nests in their dens, using grass, leaves, and twigs, but a few slept on bare dirt. And some denning bears observed in early spring were lying on wet, muddy ground.

THE LONG SLEEP

As a species, the American black bear was born sometime during the Pleistocene ice age, so its evolution has been shaped by seasonal cold and associated food shortages, as well as forest life. One adaptation is the bear's thick coat. Others are its bulky body and ability to store large amounts of fat. But its most marvelous mechanism is hibernation.

Many northern mammals—ground squirrels, marmots, wood-chucks, chipmunks, bats—enter a deep sleep to survive winter's dearth of food. But bears have evolved hibernatory mechanisms unlike any other creature.

Alaska's black bears and brown bears may den for more than half of each year, without the need to defecate, urinate, eat, or drink throughout this entire period. Yet unlike rodent hibernators, which enter a death-like torpor, their body temperature and metabolic rates drop only slightly. By winter's end they may lose 25 to 50 percent of their body weight; but for healthy bears, the loss is all, or nearly all, fat. And they show no recognizable signs of muscle atrophy or bone degeneration.

Even more extraordinary is the fact that pregnant bears give birth during this extended period of fasting and then nurse their cubs for several months while still in hibernation. The cycle of ursine pregnancy begins with midsummer mating (at age 4 or older for Alaska's black bears). Through a mechanism called delayed implantation, fertilized eggs remain detached from the female's uterus until early winter, thus delaying embryo development by

A black bear stands in an alder patch and marks branches.

several months. If a female hasn't added enough fat to get herself and a litter of cubs through the winter, the pregnancy is terminated.

After a two-month gestation period, between one and six black bear cubs are born in January or February. In Alaska, litters with more than three cubs are rare; the usual size is two. About the size of a chipmunk, newborn black bear cubs are toothless, sightless, and nearly naked, and weigh $\frac{1}{2}$ pound. They're born at an early stage of development for a good reason: by feeding on the mother's protein- and fat-rich milk, cubs place fewer demands on Mom's energy reserves than if they had remained fetuses. The den acts as a kind of surrogate womb, providing warmth and protection.

Upon giving birth, the mother licks her newborns and eats the afterbirth to keep the den clean and eliminate odors that might attract predators. The precautions are well taken: grizzlies, humans, and even wolves are known to kill and eat hibernating black bears. For similar reasons, Mom periodically awakens to eat the cubs' feces and lick up their urine. By consuming her cubs' waste, she also recovers some of the fluids lost by nursing.

Among the more intriguing studies of Alaska's hibernating black bears were those done in the early 1990s by Brian Barnes and others in the University of Alaska's Institute of Arctic Biology. Among the findings: despite outside temperatures that fell to –58°F, the sleeping bears' core temperature never dropped below 86°. Moreover, core body temperatures showed multiday rhythms in which they would cool to 86°, then rewarm, and gradually cool again. Exactly how the bears kept their body temperature from falling below 86°, and how they rewarmed themselves, remains a mystery.

The hibernating bears spent 90 percent of their time asleep. From January through March, they awakened only during a week of severe cold and when researchers made noises outside the den to test the bears' alertness. Other hibernators, such as ground squirrels, periodically rouse themselves and bring heart rates and body temperatures back to normal. Bears apparently don't need to.

THE YOUNG BEARS

When a black bear mother and her family finally leave their den in spring, the cubs will have gained 4 to 8 pounds. And by summer's end, they'll weigh in the neighborhood of 30 pounds—if they survive. Anywhere from 30 to 45 percent of Alaska's black bear cubs die before their first birthday. Some starve. Others drown, fall from trees, or get eaten by wolves, lynx, or other bears. While cannibalism by other black bears occurs, it doesn't appear common; grizzlies are a much greater threat.

Black bear cubs are normally weaned when they're $1\frac{1}{2}$ years old, sooner than either grizzlies or polar bears. But in Northern Alaska, many females apparently keep their cubs an extra year, perhaps to help them survive in a more severe climate.

Learning to live without Mom is an imposing task, and mortality rates for newly weaned black bear adolescents approach that for first-year cubs. Those skilled or lucky enough to reach adulthood face few dangers besides grizzlies and humans, and some survive into their 20s. Most, however, don't make it past their mid-teens.

Though they may become wanderers when first separated from Mom, black bears, like others of their kind, eventually settle into home ranges, where they'll spend the rest of their days. Females generally remain within their mother's home range, while males disperse widely. Because they travel into unfamiliar territory inhabited by other bears or humans, many male adolescents die before establishing a home range.

Range sizes vary greatly throughout Alaska: some are as small as 1 to 2 square miles, others exceed 200 square miles. Male black bears, like their grizzly counterparts, inhabit a much larger area than females, for both breeding and feeding purposes. The smallest are those occupied by females with newborn cubs.

Like polar bears and brown bears, black bears will display some social behaviors in the form of play, limited family ties (mainly between mother and cubs, until weaning), and occasional group feeds.

FUTURE OF THE BLACK BEAR

Alaska's black bear population is in very good shape because of the species' large numbers, its adaptability to humans, and an

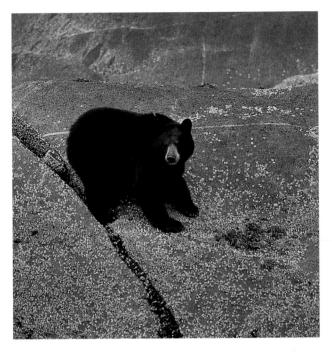

A black bear forages on barnacles and other intertidal foods.

abundance of habitat. Hunting is regulated to maintain a healthy population. Poaching for black bear parts, such as gall bladders and bear paws, has not been a problem in Alaska as it has in Asia, parts of Canada, and the Lower 48, though recently there has been some evidence of black bear poaching in Southeast Alaska. Strong penalties for poaching are necessary to minimize illegal killing.

Alaska remains blessed with expansive forested areas that provide the cover and food black bears need to thrive, so the species is under no immediate threat. But biologists warn against complacency in the future, especially in developed areas, where conflicts between land use by humans and use by bears will be the greatest. ■

VIEWING ALASKA'S BEARS

^^^

As growing numbers of people participate in adventure travel and wildlife watching, thousands visit Alaska's backcountry each summer hoping to see bears. They can be viewed throughout most of the state, from May through September, but some areas naturally offer better opportunities than others.

One of the most popular places to view grizzlies is Denali National Park, where they are frequently seen by summer visitors who are traveling the park road on shuttle and tour buses. Increasing numbers of commercial operators conduct brown bear–viewing programs in Kodiak National Wildlife Refuge and along Katmai National Park's outer coast (check with the managers of those refuge and park lands for more information). Backcountry travelers are likely to see brown/grizzly bears— preferably from a distance—in many of Alaska's protected wild- lands, including Glacier Bay and Wrangell–St. Elias National Parks, Tongass and Chugach National Forests, and the Arctic National Wildlife Refuge.

Black bears tend to be more secretive than brown bears, and therefore less visible, though they occasionally show up along trails and roads in many Alaska regions.

Polar bears are seen even less frequently, as they prefer the seldom-visited pack ice and arctic shores. Alaska, alas, has no place like Canada's Cape Churchill where polar bears congregate.

PRIME VIEWING SITES

Bears by nature tend to lead solitary lives. Adult males, in particular, are loners that seldom engage in social behavior, except during mating season. For bears to gather in large numbers and in close quarters is therefore exceptional. That they might do so while viewed by humans is even more amazing, given their natural wariness. Yet each summer, in scattered areas throughout Alaska's southern coastal regions, bears do come together in large groups. What draws them together and demands their tolerance of each other—and in some instances, of a human audience—is an abundant, concentrated, and energy-rich food source: salmon.

Of the hundreds of Alaska salmon streams where bears congregate, a few have become places where people gather as well. They come to watch, take photographs, and spend time in the company of creatures symbolic of Alaska's wildness. A couple of bear-viewing sites were established in Southeast Alaska in the early 1900s, but they attracted few people. Not until McNeil River State Game Sanctuary gained widespread acclaim in the 1970s and 1980s as a place for nonscientists to observe "bears being bears" did the public begin actively seeking out these special sites.

Over the past 10 to 15 years, four of Alaska's wild places have become especially well known for their bear-viewing programs. At most of these sites, people come to see brown bears. A notable exception is Anan Creek, known for its black bears.

Because bears at these sites have become habituated to humans, they sometimes wander close enough that you can smell their dank fur, hear the loud crunching as they tear at salmon flesh and bone, see the scars that streak their faces and bodies, hear their panting breaths. It's closer than you'd ever want to get while

One of the most popular places to see grizzlies is Denali National Park.

exploring the wilderness on your own; but here, watching from a viewing platform or accompanied by knowledgeable guides, it's safe to watch, listen, enjoy—as long as you obey the rules. These are still wild animals.

The nature of these places and the way they're managed vary greatly. But as McNeil's longtime manager, Larry Aumiller, says, all of them teach a critically important lesson: when things are done right, bears and humans can indeed peacefully coexist.

■ **McNEIL RIVER.** The McNeil River State Game Sanctuary is the standard by which all other bear-viewing areas are measured. Established in 1967 and managed by the state's Division of Wildlife Conservation, this sanctuary on the Alaska Peninsula protects the world's largest gathering of brown bears.

The focal point of the gathering is McNeil Falls, where bears come to feed on chum salmon. During the peak of that

July–August chum run, dozens of brown bears congregate. As many as 144 individual bears (adults and cubs) have been identi- fied along the river in a single season. And in July 1997, biologists counted 70 bears at the falls at one time.

Even more impressive than the numbers of bears, perhaps, is their acceptance of a human presence. "Think about it," says Larry Aumiller, McNeil's manager since 1976. "You've got this group of 11 or 12 people standing in the middle of 40, 50, 60 bears. You're very close to where they want to be. And they tolerate you." Some will eat salmon, take naps, nurse cubs, or even mate within a short distance of the visitor viewing pads.

A key ingredient of McNeil's success is people management. Only 10 people per day, accompanied by one or two sanctuary guides, are allowed to visit McNeil Falls. Once there, bear watchers are restricted to a defined viewing area. And they keep to a set

---■---

Photographers take aim at a brown bear in McNeil River sanctuary.

schedule. In this way, people become predictable to the bears. The other crucial element: McNeil's bears view humans as neutral objects. People don't pose a threat, nor are they a source of food.

Until the mid-1980s, few people visited the sanctuary before July 1. But a new pattern emerged when a June sockeye run began to increase dramatically at Mikfik Creek, a small neighboring stream of McNeil River. Not surprisingly, more and more bears were lured by Mikfik's improved fishing opportunities—and following the bears were wildlife photographers. Mikfik's popularity prompted the state to expand its permit period, which now runs from early June through late August.

While Mikfik has made the sanctuary's bear-viewing more diverse, McNeil Falls remains the primary focus in July and August. A mile above McNeil's mouth, it's a step-like series of small waterfalls, pools, and rapids. Individual bears take up fishing positions based on their place in the ursine pecking order. Prime spots are located along the western bank, opposite the two viewing pads. Here the most dominant bears—adult males, some weighing 1,000 pounds or more—jockey for position.

The bears use a variety of fishing techniques. Some stand motionless, patiently monitoring the river. When a chum swims by, the bear pins it to the stream bottom with its paws, then bites it. Others use snorkeling techniques, and a few even dive for fish. The chum run ends by mid- to late August, but the bears begin to disperse even before then, as they go in search of another nutritious food: berries.

Getting there: The McNeil River State Game Sanctuary is on the upper Alaska Peninsula, 250 miles southwest of Anchorage. Most visitors fly in, using floatplane services based in Homer.

Manager: Alaska Department of Fish and Game.

Prime viewing: June through mid-August.

Visitor limits: Ten people, accompanied by sanctuary staff, per day. Permit applications must be received by March 1; winners are determined by lottery.

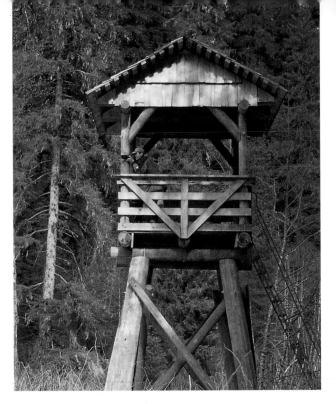

Visitors can watch bears from a viewing tower at Pack Creek.

Overnight facilities: Spaces provided for tent camping.

Information: Alaska Department of Fish and Game, Division of Wildlife Conservation, 333 Raspberry Road, Anchorage, AK 99518-1599; (907) 267-2182.

■ **PACK CREEK.** Admiralty Island, within Tongass National Forest in Southeast Alaska, has long been recognized as an important brown bear refuge. The Tlingit people who first lived here called it *kootznoowoo,* "fortress of the bears"—a fitting description for one of North America's richest bear habitats.

Ninety-six miles long, with 678 miles of coastline, dozens of salmon streams, and forested mountains, Admiralty Island is home to 1,700 bears: about one for each of its 1,644 square miles. Few places in the world have higher densities.

On the east side of Admiralty is Pack Creek, the region's premier bear-watching site. Pack Creek's special niche can be traced to the early 1930s, when the drainage was closed to bear hunting (a closure that has since been expanded). One year later, the Civilian Conservation Corps built a platform above the creek to aid bear-viewing.

Still, Pack Creek had few bears until Stan Price settled there in the mid-1950s. Nicknamed Stan the Bear Man, Price became a local legend because of his unusual friendship with bears. He took in several orphaned cubs and raised them as pets. And contrary to state regulations, he fed bears on his homestead. Inevitably the number of bears grew. Price died in 1989, but the bears have remained. Today 30 to 35 brown bears use Pack Creek, though only the most tolerant ones are seen by visitors.

The site is now managed as a day-use area, and visitors must store and eat their food at a designated picnic area. Following a safety talk, permit holders are turned loose, though viewing options are limited: bear-watching is allowed only at a sand spit near the creek mouth and an upstream observation tower, both reached by well-defined paths. The presence of 5 or 6 bears at one time is considered a good viewing day.

Getting there: Pack Creek is on Admiralty Island, within Tongass National Forest, 25 miles south of Juneau. It can be reached by either boat or air.

Manager: Alaska Department of Fish and Game and U.S. Forest Service.

Prime viewing: Mid-July through late August.

Visitor limits: Twenty-four people per day during the peak period of July 5 to August 25; permits and reservations issued on a first-come, first-served basis beginning March 1 each year. Permits are also required during the nonpeak periods from June 1 to July 4 and from August 26 to September 10, but reservations aren't required and there is no visitor cap, though groups are restricted to 12 people.

Overnight facilities: None.

Information: Admiralty Island National Monument, 8461 Old Dairy Road, Juneau, AK 99801; (907) 586-8790.

■ **ANAN CREEK.** Each summer, as they do in forest streams throughout Southeast Alaska, dozens of bears fish Anan Creek for salmon. What's different here is that both brown and black bears use the creek; normally, blacks tend to avoid the larger and more aggressive browns.

Even more unusual, from a bear-viewing perspective, is the fact that the black bears are the chief attraction at the Anan Creek Bear Observatory. They're easily observed during the daylight hours, while Anan's brown bears are rarely seen except early in the morning or late at night.

Anan Creek, in Tongass National Forest, has been locally known for its gathering of black bears since the early 1900s. Each summer, as many as 30 to 40 black bears are drawn here by a run of more than 100,000 pink salmon. Working among moss-covered granite boulders that border the tea-colored stream, bears grab their prey from pools along the shore.

Upon catching a fish, most of Anan's black bears retreat into the creekside boulder piles or scurry into the thick forest understory. It's uncommon to see more than a handful at any one time, but bear researchers say that Anan is nevertheless one of the best spots in North America to watch *Ursus americanus.*

A viewing platform was first built at Anan in the 1930s, but the creek required only minimal management until the 1990s, when annual visitation jumped from fewer than 1,000 to nearly 4,000 people. In response, the Forest Service has put a number of restrictions into place, including a prohibition on food beyond the trailhead. As at Pack Creek, visitors are allowed to walk the trails unescorted. The principal viewing site is a wooden-decked and partly roofed platform that overlooks the creek and falls, which tumble through a narrow, forest-enclosed gorge.

Getting there: The Anan Creek Bear Observatory is in Southeast Alaska's Tongass National Forest, about 30 miles southeast of Wrangell. It's accessible by either boat or floatplane.

Manager: U.S. Forest Service.

Prime viewing: July through early September.

Visitor limits: No daily limit, but viewing groups are limited to 8 people or fewer at a time; permits are required for commercial guided groups.

Overnight facilities: A public-use cabin is located about a mile from the observatory; it must be reserved. No camping is permitted in the area.

Information: U.S. Forest Service, Wrangell Ranger District, P.O. Box 51, Wrangell, AK 99929; (907) 874-2323.

■ **BROOKS FALLS.** The ritual begins in early July, with the return of the sockeyes. Thousands of bright silvery fish enter the Brooks River and push their way upstream toward spawning grounds in Brooks Lake. Nearing the end of their journey from the sea, they face one final obstacle: a 6-foot-high falls. Hundreds of sockeyes school in the pool below as they wait their turn to jump.

Following the salmon to Brooks Falls are brown bears. A dozen or more may congregate here in July, grabbing sockeye from atop the falls, snorkeling in the pools below, or watching from stream banks, waiting for scraps. Also watching are 30 people, squeezed together on an elevated platform built along the river's south shore. By summer's end, more than 12,000 people from around the world will visit.

A 1^1/$_2$ -mile-long clearwater stream that connects Brooks and Naknek Lakes, the Brooks River is located within 4-million-acre Katmai National Park and Preserve. Over the past 15 years, this

Alaska Peninsula stream has evolved into one of the state's premier bear-viewing sites. Bears often fish within 50 feet of the viewing platform. They may also be seen on the lower river (from a second platform) or even in Brooks Camp, a nearby developed area that includes a lodge, cabins, visitor center, and campground.

Brooks Camp got its start in 1950 as a sportfishing destination. Then it was rare to see bears along the Brooks River because they were chased away or shot, first by Native inhabitants of the region and later by anglers. A dramatic, albeit gradual change occurred when the National Park Service began to actively manage the area in the 1950s. Within three decades Brooks Camp was transformed from a little-known fisherman's paradise into a world-renowned bear-watcher's haven. Nowadays, at the peak of the July salmon run, as many as 35 to 40 brown bears inhabit the Brooks River drainage.

Visitors must obey a series of rules, but for the most part they're free to roam. As many as 300 people pass through the Brooks Falls platforms daily, including day-trippers who fly in for a few hours of bear-watching. Park managers, concerned about adverse human impacts, have proposed some changes. The number of day visitors may eventually be capped, and visitor facilities may some day be moved to the north side of the Brooks River, where they're expected to be less disruptive.

Getting there: Brooks Falls and nearby Brooks Camp are in Katmai National Park and Preserve, 300 miles southwest of Anchorage. Most visitors fly, via commercial airline, to King Salmon, then take a floatplane to Brooks.

Manager: National Park Service.

Prime viewing: July and September.

Visitor limits: There are plans to limit day-use visitation.

Overnight facilities: Brooks Lodge, owned by Katmailand, Inc., of Anchorage, (800) 544-0551. There's also a Park Service campground; sites must be reserved.

Information: Katmai National Park, P.O. Box 7, King Salmon, AK 99613; (907) 246-3305.

SUGGESTED READING

Bledsoe, Thomas. *Brown Bear Summer: Life Among Alaska's Giants.* New York: Truman Talley Books, 1987.

Craighead, Frank C. *Track of the Grizzly.* San Francisco: Sierra Club Books, 1979.

Davids, Richard C., and Dan Guravich. *Lords of the Arctic: A Journey Among the Polar Bears.* New York: Macmillan Publishing Co., 1982.

Dewey, Donald. *Bears.* New York: Gallery Books, 1991.

Dufresne, Frank. *No Room for Bears.* Seattle: Alaska Northwest Books, 1991.

Fair, Jeff. *The Great American Bear.* Minocqua, Wis.: Northward Press, 1990.

Herrero, Stephen. *Bear Attacks: Their Causes and Avoidance.* New York: Nick Lyons Books, 1985.

Illingworth, Frank. *Wild Life Beyond the North.* New York: Charles Scribner's Sons, 1952.

Lopez, Barry. *Arctic Dreams: Imagination and Desire in a Northern Landscape.* New York: Charles Scribner's Sons, 1986.

Lynch, Wayne. *Bears: Monarchs of the Northern Wilderness.* Seattle: The Mountaineers, 1993.

McNamee, Thomas. *The Grizzly Bear.* New York: Alfred A. Knopf, 1984.

Murie, Adolph. *The Grizzlies of Mount McKinley.* Seattle: University of Washington Press, 1985.

Murray, John A., ed. *The Great Bear: Contemporary Writings on the Grizzly.* Seattle: Alaska Northwest Books, 1992.

Nelson, Richard. *Hunters of the Northern Ice.* Chicago: The University of Chicago Press, 1969.

———. *Make Prayers to the Raven: A Koyukon View of the Northern Forest.* Chicago: The University of Chicago Press, 1983.

Perry, Richard. *The World of the Polar Bear.* Seattle: University of Washington Press, 1966.

Rennick, Penny, ed. *Alaska's Bears.* Anchorage: Alaska Geographic Society, 1993.

Rennicke, Jeff. *Bears of Alaska in Life and Legend.* Boulder, Colo.: Roberts Rinehart Publishers, 1987.

Rockwell, David. *Giving Voice to Bear: Northern American Indian Myths, Rituals, and Images of Bear.* Niwot, Colo.: Roberts Rinehart Publishers, 1991.

Russell, Andy. *Grizzly Country.* New York: Alfred A. Knopf, 1967.

Savage, Candace. *Grizzly Bears.* San Francisco: Sierra Club Books, 1990.

Seton, Ernest Thompson. *The Biography of a Grizzly.* New York: Grosset and Dunlap, 1899.

Shephard, Paul, and Barry Sanders. *The Sacred Paw: The Bear in Nature, Myth, and Literature.* New York: Penguin Books, 1985.

Smith, Dave. *Backcountry Bear Basics: The Definitive Guide to Avoiding Unpleasant Encounters.* Seattle: The Mountaineers, 1997.

Stirling, Ian, ed. *Bears: Majestic Creatures of the Wild.* Emmaus, Penn.: Rodale Press, 1993.

Stirling, Ian, and Dan Guravich. *Polar Bears.* Ann Arbor: University of Michigan Press, 1990.

Walker, Tom, and Larry Aumiller. *River of Bears.* Stillwater, Minn.: Voyageur Press, 1993.

INDEX

*Page numbers in **bold face** indicate illustrations.*

INDEX

INDEX

Alaska Northwest Books™ is proud to publish another book in
its Alaska Pocket Guide series, designed with the curious
traveler in mind. Ask for more books in this series at your
favorite bookstore, or contact Alaska Northwest Books™.

ALASKA NORTHWEST BOOKS™

An imprint of Graphic Arts Center Publishing Company
P.O. Box 10306, Portland, OR 97296-0306
800-452-3032